SUPERBASE 4
DECI

SUPERBASE 4

DECI

NATO's European Air Combat Range

Chuck Stewart

Published in 1988 by Osprey Publishing
Limited
27A Floral Street, London WC2E 9DP
Member company of the George Philip
Group

British Library Cataloguing in Publication
Data

Stewart, Chuck
    Deci: NATO's European air combat
    range.
    1. North Atlantic Treaty Organization
    air forces. Military aircraft—
    Illustrations
    I. Title   II. Series
    623.74'6'091821
ISBN 0-85045-886-2

Editor Dennis Baldry
Designed by David Tarbutt
Printed in Hong Kong

Front cover A No 92 Sqn
Phantom FGR.2 wearing the old-
style RAF green and grey
camouflage, large insignia and
fuselage flash. One of 120
modified F-4Ms delivered to
RAF Strike Command XV490 is
based at Wildenrath in West
Germany

Title pages With its short,
razor-like wings, the F-104
hardly looks the part of the
classic ground attack aircraft,
but of the eight wings still flying
them in the Italian Air Force, half
are tactical strike units. This 5th
Stormo F-104S (MM6756) is
ready for departure with a pair
of multi-rocket launchers on the
inboard pylons

For those who flew their last mission at Deci.

Right Self-portrait of the author in one of Flight Systems' F-100s high above the Mediterranean during a dart-tow mission . . . no small chore while pulling +5Gs in a descending left turn with a flight of F-15s making live-firing passes in your six o'clock. The strain shows

Because Deci is a quadra-national NATO base operated by the Italians and shared by the British, Germans and Americans, language is sometimes a problem. In the air it's strictly English, but on the ground, as this warning sign illustrates, everything is in Italian, English and German

Introduction

Decimomannu Air Base, located at the southern end of the island of Sardinia in the Mediterranean Sea, is the busiest airbase in Europe. It can make that claim not by virtue of its size (it is actually a tiny base, with only a single 9800-foot runway, a half-dozen permanently-assigned aircraft and 2500 personnel at best), but because of its virtually one-of-a-kind training facilities, which are used by the air forces of nearly every nation in Western Europe at a rate of nearly 200 sorties per day.

Decimomannu is the home of the only Air Combat Manoeuvring Instrumentation (ACMI) range, called the 'Air Weapons Training Installation' (AWTI) by the Italian hosts, currently operating in Europe. Established in 1960 by the NATO partnership of Italy, Germany, Great Britain and Canada, the ACMI range complex includes computer-monitored airspace for the practice of dissimilar air combat training (DACT) and a manned, scorable bombing range. Though Canada was replaced as a partner by the United States, the ACMI range continues its same, ever-growing mission some 28 years later: to provide realistic air combat training to the pilots who comprise the front line of defence of Western Europe.

The complex system of airborne transmitters, ground relay stations and computer terminals that make the air-to-air portion of ACMI training so effective is operated and maintained by the Cubic Corporation of San Diego, California. Described later in the book, the system is a technological marvel that records the gut-wrenching, adrenalin-pumping, speed-blurred hyper-action of a dogfight and presents it as a training experience that can be rationally analysed after the fact to teach a pilot the strengths and weaknesses that could make the ultimate difference in combat.

Since Italy, Germany, Great Britain and the US each rotate a different squadron of aircraft into Deci every 3 to 5 weeks, the number and variety of aircraft deployed there in a year is incredible. With the generous cooperation of the Italian Air Force hosts as well as the maintenance personnel of the deployed units, all the photographs in this book were taken at Decimomannu between September 1985 and October 1986, using Pentax LM and Nikon F-3 cameras and Kodachrome 64 film.

Chuck Stewart is a highly-respected aviation photographer and historian from California whose work has appeared in numerous publications. His first book for Osprey was *Superbase 3: RAMSTEIN*.

Contents

Resident
Italian units

Hardly a pot of gold, this
dilapidated T-6 trainer in the
Deci junkyard is all that waits at
the end of a double rainbow
arcing over the base

Sitting alone at one end of the
Deci junkyard, which is piled
high with wrecked Fiat G.91Ts,
is this T-6G Texan advanced
trainer, retired in the early
seventies. Though unidentified,
it still wears the standard Italian
'training-orange' livery and the
Matricola Militare number
MM54099

This nearly-mint condition photo-reconnaissance RT-33A never moves from this spot and is rumoured to be in storage for eventual display, though there is already a T-33 at the main gate. The black and yellow-striped underside is typical for a photo-recon bird, but the emblem on the tail indicates this T-bird last flew with the 51st *Stormo*, a strike unit based at Istrana

Though Deci holds the distinction of being the busiest military airfield in Europe, there are only six aircraft permanently assigned to the base, two of them search and rescue helicopters. This is one of the four others, an Aermacchi MB.326 from 'CSSTA,' a one-of-a-kind training unit specially-created for Deci to provide rated staff officers with enough proficiency training to maintain their currency

This Agusta-Bell 212, the licence-built version of the UH-1N, wears the standard Italian high-visibility SAR livery. Detached from 670 Sqn, it displays its Deci-exclusive callsign, 'AWTI (Air Weapons Training Installation) 02' on the fuselage

Italian visitors

Considered by many to be the world's most exciting aerobatic team, Italy's 'Frecce Tricolori' flies an impressive and colourful routine with 9-plane formations backed up by two ebullient soloists. Their Aermacchi MB.339s are painted bright blue with patriotic Italian tri-colours underneath and equally patriotic smoke trailing behind. On the occasion of the 25th anniversary of the Decimomannu AWTI in September 1985, the Frecce Tricolori were the featured performers at the base's first airshow in a decade. Based at Rivolto with the 313th *Gruppo*, the team made its first appearance outside Europe during the summer-87 airshow season in the US and was a huge success

This Aermacchi MB.326 visited
Deci on a weekend cross-
country trip from its home base
at Cameri. The tail and fuselage
emblems identify it as belonging
to the 53rd *Stormo*, 653rd
Gruppo, where it is used as a
proficiency trainer and
squadron hack

This orange and white
Aermacchi MB.339 from the
Reporto Sperimentale di Volo
(RSV), a special flight research
and development unit based at
Pratica di Mare, visits Deci
several times a year to perform
radio and NAVAID calibration
checks. Note the rear seat filled
with measuring equipment

Flying as wingman for the
orange and white flight check
aircraft was another Aermacchi
MB.339 from the RSV unit, this
one in more typical training
markings

Lineup of Fiat (now Aeritalia) G.91T/1s on the Deci ramp. The crest on the tails is that of the 60th *Stormo*, the Italian Air Force's advanced jet training wing from Foggia-Amendola. Because of Sardinian's ideal weather, there are only four small maintenance hangars at Deci, so all aircraft are kept outside, lined wingtip-to-wingtip along a mile and a quarter length of parking ramp

Inset A Fiat G.91T/1 of the 60th *Stormo* taxies by on its way to bombing practice at Capa Frasca range northwest of Deci. The G.91 normally carries only one blue 4-kg practice bomb on each underwing pylon

A 60th *Stormo* G.91T ready for a practice bombing mission

Developed from the G.91R and T-models and built from 1971 to 1976, the more-powerful Fiat G.91Y single-seat light attack aircraft is armed with two 30 mm DEFA 552 cannons in the nose and four underwing pylons for a variety of ordnance. This sharkmouth example from the 32nd *Stormo*, 13th *Gruppo*, at Brindisi, is carrying four practice bombs

An early Fiat G.91R strike and reconnaissance aircraft wearing the tail badge of the 2nd *Stormo* from Treviso. The R-model G.91 is powered by a single Rolls-Royce Orpheus engine and armed with four 0.5 inch Colt-Browning machine guns in the nose

Off for a dogfight on the ACMI range, this F-104S (MM6934) of the 5th *Stormo*, 23rd *Gruppo*, a strike/interceptor squadron from Rimini, is carrying a pylon-mounted instrumentation pod that simulates an AIM-9 Sidewinder missile and transmits aircraft performance data to a computer system and radar intercept controller on the ground. 'Live' data, including altitude, airspeed, turn and bank, climb and descent, G-load, weapons status and gunsight picture, is transmitted by the instrumentation pod and recorded by a huge bank of computers that synthesize the information into a graphic 3-dimensional playback of the mission that is used to score the fight and debrief the pilots, a'la 'Top Gun'

COME VELTRI CH'USCISSER DI CATENA

23

Above With his arm casually draped over the side of the cockpit, this pilot taxies his F-104 back after a bombing mission to Capa Frasca. This Aeritalia-built F-104S (MM6848) now wears the emblems of the 5th *Stormo* and 102nd *Gruppo* from Rimini, though it previously flew with the RSV test unit as RS-04

Left The squadron badge of the 23rd *Gruppo* is a greyhound jumping over a Sidewinder missile

Above This very clean F-104S (MM6849), carrying a wingtip-mounted ACMI instrumentation pod, is from the 9th *Stormo*, 10th *Gruppo*, an interceptor unit based at Grazzanise. Because of the close proximity of the ACMI range and the ruggedness of the manoeuvres involved in dogfighting, F-104s do not fly their Deci air combat missions with the usual tip-tanks. As a result, their endurance on internal fuel is a very short 40 minutes. On the tail is the famous 'Cavallino Rampante' emblem of the 10th *Gruppo*, honouring Major Francesco Baracca, the Italian ace who first used the emblem on his SPAD XIII in WWI

Above right Taxying out for a mission on the ACMI range, this F-104S (MM6976) wears the subdued markings of the Trapani-based 37th *Stormo*, 18th *Gruppo*, on the intake. On the rear fuselage is a white thistle 'zap' marking from No 1 Sqn of the Belgian Air Force

Right This unusual powder-blue F-104S (MM6945) appropriately wears 'ASA' (*Aggiornamento Sistema Arma*) titles and the emblem of the *Reporto Sperimentale di Volo* flight test unit from Pratica di Mare for its role as the testbed for an Aeritalia-sponsored weapon system test programme conducted at Deci. Note the Selenia Aspide (modified Sparrow) radar-guided air-to-air missiles on the underwing pylons

The Tornado was designed and built specifically for a tri-national requirement for a multi-role combat aircraft by the British Aerospace, Messerschmitt-Bolkow-Blohm and Aeritalia cooperative named Panavia. This lineup of Tornado strike aircraft wears the yellow lightning bolt of the 156th *Gruppo* through the eagle emblem of the 36th *Stormo* on the tail. When they converted from F-104s in 1985, 156th *Gruppo*, based at Gioia del Colle, was the second unit in the Italian Air Force to be equipped with the Tornado

Representing the first Italian Air Force unit to be equipped with the Tornado is this Tornado IDS (interdiction/strike variant), wearing the 6th *Stormo* red devil insignia and 155th *Gruppo* blue flashes on the tail. Based at Ghedi, the 155th *Gruppo* and its sister squadron, the 154th, are tasked with Italy's nuclear strike mission

A pair of 6th *Stormo* 'Red Devil' Tornados with the red fin flash of the 154th *Gruppo* from Ghedi. Since the four nations permanently based at Deci have only one small hangar each, all but the most major maintenance is performed outside on the line

The Italian partner in the Panavia Tornado programme, Aeritalia, maintains a flight test facility at Deci to evaluate a variety of ordnance and electronics for its F-104s and Tornados. This Tornado (MM7075) came to Deci straight from the production line in Turin before delivery and application of unit markings

Operating from Aeritalia's Deci flight test facility for most of 1986 was the colourful X-586, the fifth prototype Tornado, the first built by Aeritalia in 1975. Though painted in standard air force camouflage instead of its earlier white and orange livery and bearing remnants of 156th *Gruppo* squadron markings on the tail and intake, this hard-working Tornado also wears orange prototype bands, the tri-national Panavia insignia and white photo-reference markings. In this case, the photo-reference markings were used as measuring points to aid in evaluating the performance of new missiles being test-fired on the range. Mounted in photo-pods on the centreline and outboard wing pylon are the high-speed cameras that record the launch

Another prototype being flown at Deci during 1986 was the joint Italian-Brazilian project, the Aeritalia-Aermacchi-Embraer AMX strike aircraft. Though it normally made long straight-in approaches to land, on the last day of its stay at Deci, the test pilot showed what the little fighter could do, with several low-level, high-speed passes and an overhead approach with a 90-degree pitch-out that pulled vapour trails and at least +6Gs. Delivery of the first production AMX for the Italian Air Force is scheduled for mid-1988

Originally designed as an executive jet along the lines of the Learjet, the Piaggio-Douglas PD.808 never caught on in the civil market, but found a home in the Italian Air Force flying liaison, ECM and radio calibration missions. This example is from the 14th *Stormo*, 8th *Gruppo*, at Pratica di Mare

The heart of the Italian Air Force Transport Command is the 46th Air Brigade at Pisa, which consists of two squadrons (*Gruppi*) of Aeritalia G.222 tactical transports and one squadron of C-130s. This C-130H from the 50th *Gruppo* wears the older transport livery of white upper surfaces on natural metal

With its props in reverse pitch and a spotter watching from the rear cargo ramp, another 46th *Aerobrigata*, 50th *Gruppo*, C-130H displays the newer-style tactical camouflage as it backs off of the 'hot' cargo pad

Flight Systems' F-100s

Under a long-term contract with the US Air Force, Flight Systems Inc of Mojave, California, maintains a fleet of six F-100F Super Sabres in Europe, normally with two at Hurn in the UK and four at Deci. They provide their own aircraft, pilots and maintenance, and fly a very demanding schedule of aerial dart-towing missions so that USAF pilots can sharpen their skills with live-fire gunnery practice, a valuable training experience not available in the crowded airspace over mainland Europe. N417FS undergoes engine checks

Inset One of the aluminium foil-covered plywood darts is attached to a Flight Systems F-100. The dart is carried on a special pylon under the port wing that contains a spool of high-strength cable used to reel the aerodynamic dart out to 'fly' at a safe distance (1200–1500 feet) behind the tow plane. Occasionally the dart is damaged and starts to spin, or is completely shot away from the cable. In that case, instead of reeling it back in for scoring on the ground, the entire cable is cut at the pylon by means of a steel blade driven by a shotgun shell and allowed to fall into the sea

Below The Flight Systems F-100 fleet at Deci: N417FS, 418FS, 416FS and 414FS. FSI's F-100Fs are resurrected from the inventory of nearly 175 retired Super Sabres in storage at the Davis-Monthan AFB Aerospace Maintenance and Regeneration Unit, better known simply as 'the boneyard'

Aggressor F-5Es

One of the semi-regular tenants at Deci is a flight of six F-5Es that, along with pilots and maintenance personnel, rotate bi-monthly from the 527th Aggressor Squadron at RAF Alconbury. Flying three and four gut-wrenching sorties per day, the Aggressors are the resident instructors for the practical course at the Decimomannu graduate school of dissimilar air combat. This is a formal portrait of 01534 holding short of the runway awaiting takeoff clearance

This F-5E (01545) wears a
replacement rudder and one of
the more colourful Aggressor
camouflage schemes of 3-tone
blue

With its tailhook down and
locked into a restraining device,
the two 5000-lb thrust General
Electric J85-21A engines of the
desert-camouflaged 01553
undergo power checks at one of
Deci's heavily-used run-up pads

01568 waiting to go

Though it only happened twice in the last decade, it actually snowed at Deci in March 1986, covering everything on the ramp, including this Agressor F-5, with an inch of snow that lasted barely past sunrise

USAF Eagles

Roosting under a classic Mediterranean sky scattered with towering
cumulus clouds, a lineup of F-15Cs from the Bitburg-based 22nd TFS,
36th TFW. Probably the most frequent visitors to Deci, the Bitburg
Eagles never fail to impress with their finely-honed professional
performance on the ground and in the air. Their maintenance
personnel literally stunned a visiting delegation of Swiss Air Force
mechanics when they performed a complete F-15 engine swap in
only 45-minutes

Inset The colourful F-15C of the 36th TFW commander at Bitburg.
The red, white and blue markings commemorate those originally
applied to the F-100Cs of the 'Skyblazers,' an aerobatic team formed
by the 36th TFW at Bitburg in 1960. Though these striking markings
were very popular with spotters and airshow audiences and added a
much-needed dash of colour to the usually-drab F-15, they were
removed during the summer of 1987

Right After a quick walk-around inspection at the 'last chance,' the maintenance team pulls the chocks and salutes, signalling this Bitburg F-15C is ready to go

Above With yet another thunderstorm lingering in the distance, the F-15C of the 32nd TFS commander from Soesterberg rests beside the joint USAF-RAF-Flight Systems hangar. The colourful 'Wolfhounds' emblem on the nose of 79-032 has since been toned-down to a black silhouette

Major Joe Gentile

Like father, like son. Major Joe Gentile, who visited Deci while flying F-16s with the 401st TFW at Torrejon, is the son of WW 2 ace Don Gentile, who, in his P-51B, *Shangri-La*, was credited with 19½ aerial victories over Europe. Maj Gentile is following the footsteps of the son of another WW 2 ace, Francis Gabreski, and is now flying F-16s with the 86th TFW at Ramstein

USAF transports

The cargo version of the Short Brothers 330 regional airliner, eighteen C-23A Sherpas were delivered to the 10th MAS, 322nd MAW, at Zweibrucken during 1985. Derided as the slowest and ugliest plane in the inventory, the C-23 has nonetheless proven its mettle as a light transport ferrying priority aircraft parts and engines throughout the European theatre. Each Sherpa is named after a different USAFE base; *Bitburg*, above, makes thrice-weekly trips to Deci via Comiso, Sicily, hauling both passengers and cargo

Located at the southern end of the island of Sardinia, Decimomannu Air Base is supplied almost exclusively via C-130 flights from the mainland. On any Tuesday or Thursday afternoon, it would not be unusual to see half a dozen C-130s from 3 or 4 different countries lined up on the cargo ramp. This is a MAC C-130E from the 314th TAW at Little Rock AFB Arkansas, wearing European One camouflage with a touch of black

This 1964-model C-130E is from the 37th TAS, 435th TAW, at Rhein-Main and wears the seldom-seen desert camouflage. The USAF C-130s that fly the Deci resupply missions, nicknamed 'Eagle Flights', are rotated from stateside MAC and Air Guard units and normally operate out of Aviano Air Base via Comiso, Deci, Ramstein, Rhein-Main, Zaragoza and Mildenhall

An unusual visitor to Deci is this KC-130F aerial tanker from VR-22 at NAS Rota, Spain. Normally when the Navy visits, it is to schedule time on the Capa Frasca bombing range for carrier-based A-6s and A-4s who are in the area on manoeuvres

No 899 Sqn, Fleet Air Arm

When Royal Navy No 889 Sqn from Yeovilton deploys to Deci with its Sea Harriers, it brings along this pair of Hawker Hunter T.8Ms for use as proficiency trainers. These 2-seat Hunters, originally delivered to the Fleet Air Arm in 1958, were recently modified with Sea Harrier instrumentation, electronics and radar to help speed up conversion training and give check rides

Profile view of Hunter T.8M XL580 preparing for a training sortie on the ACMI range. XL580 was the first Hunter T.8 assigned to the Flag Officer Flying Training unit at RNAS Yeovilton and, some 30 years and several rebuilds later, is still working hard and looking as sleek and beautiful as ever

The Royal Navy's Sea Harrier
FRS.1, first flown in 1977, is the
logical development of the basic
RAF Harrier GR.3. It has a
completely new nose with a
raised bubble canopy and
Ferranti Blue Fox radar,
improved performance and an
all-new weapons system
package. ZD579 displays the
subdued No 899 Sqn winged-fist
emblem on the tail and carries
dual 30 mm Aden cannons in
flush-mounted fairings along the
belly

Lineup of No 899 Sqn Sea Harriers. The V/STOL Sea Harrier proved itself a highly-effective fighting machine in the Falklands War, where it earned the nickname 'the Black Death' after downing 24 Argentinian aircraft in air-to-air combat without a single loss

This nose view of a Sea Harrier
pilot strapping in shows the yaw
vane directly in front of the
canopy, a primitive yet vital
piece of equipment that
indicates wind direction when
the Harrier is in the hover mode

FRADU Hunter

This overall-grey Hunter T.8C from the Royal Navy Fleet Requirements and Direction Unit (FRADU) was flown in by the station commander of RNAS Yeovilton so he could have a 'look-see' at his 899 Sqn Sea Harriers in action. The Yeovilton Hunters are maintained exclusively by civilian contract mechanics from Airwork Services Ltd, who obviously lavish their airplanes with the care and attention these classics deserve. XE665 started life as a Hunter F.4 for the RAF, but was rebuilt as a 2-seat T.8 by Armstrong Whitworth Aircraft and became the third Hunter T.8 allocated to the Flag Officer Flying Training unit at Yeovilton

Head-on view of the FRADU Hunter T.8C, showing the nose-mounted landing light and the starboard gun blister, removed from the T.8Ms, for the single 30 mm Aden cannon

RAF air defence aircraft

This Hawker-Siddely Hawk T.1A from No. 1 Tactical Weapons Unit at RAF Brawdy is about to mix it up with the big boys, a flight of Tornado F.2s. With ACMI range rules that even some of the odds between dissimilar aircraft and make the fight a contest of pilot skill, endurance and tactics, the Hawk more than stands a chance

A lineup of Phantom F.3s from No 74 Sqn at Wattisham. During 1984, in the wake of the Falkland Islands War, 15 ex-US Marine F-4Js were brought out of storage at Davis-Monthan AFB and placed on the rolls of No 74 Sqn to cover the gap in the RAF air defence network created by the transfer of No 23 Sqn's Phantom FGR.2s to Mount Pleasant, the Falklands. In order to bring their crews up to peak combat readiness, No 74 Sqn was a frequent visitor to Deci in 1986

Right The famous 'Deci Path' that leads from the RAF maintenance operations building to the RAF ramp. Half of its length is decorated with the fuselage flashes of units that have visited Deci. In the background, the current residents, Phantom F.3s of the No 74 (Tiger) Sqn

Below One of several No 74 Sqn black-tail Phantoms, in this case ZE353, taxies out for an engagement on the ACMI range. Though big, brutish and wide in the turn, RAF Phantoms consistently receive high marks from the Aggressors for their performance

Right This No 74 Sqn Phantom F.3 sat out the September 1985 25th anniversary airshow on the back lot at Deci. Its sea-green livery is unique among RAF Phantoms

Bottom right The massive bulk and angular lines of the Phantom always photograph well, especially in the case of this nicely-marked air defence FGR.2 from No 29 Sqn, RAF Leuchars, Scotland

The crew of this 'Tiger' Phantom
looks ready for business

RAF strike/attack aircraft

A view of the RAF and USAF flightlines at Deci, featuring the Tornado GR.1s of No 17 Sqn from Bruggen, Germany, in the foreground. The stainless steel tubing of the Meyerinck-Pantograph above-ground refuelling system, installed in early-1986, is a boon for sortie turn-around, but a definite eyesore as far as photography is concerned

Left The mailed fist emblem on the tail identifies this Tornado GR.1 as one from No 17 Sqn at Bruggen. An armourer checks the 4-kg practice bombs in the two belly-mounted CBLS (carrier, bomb, light stores) containers before ZD793 taxies away

Bottom left A picturesque sky doesn't make outdoor maintenance on the scorching hot concrete ramp any more tolerable. Crews take a noontime break from preparing this GR.1 (ZA392) for a practice bombing mission. A fully-loaded Tornado IDS can carry as much as 18,000 lbs of external stores into combat

Below Head-on view of a No 16 Sqn Tornado GR.1T, showing to good advantage the full-span leading edge slats and the fully-extended double-slotted flaps

The gold star on the tail of this
Tornado GR.1 (ZD748) identifies
it as the property of No 31 Sqn,
an ex-Jaguar operator based at
Bruggen, Germany. Though the
camouflage hides it well, note
this Tornado's typical soot-
blackened rudder and vertical
stabilizer, caused by the thrust-
reverser bucket doors
deflecting the exhaust onto the
tail

Laarbruch-based No 16 Squadron's famous 'The Saint' emblem adorns this lineup of Tornado GR.1Ts. Tornados began replacing the Buccaneers of RAF Germany in 1982, but No 16 Squadron's mission remains the same: low-level strike

Left This Jaguar GR.1 of No 41 Sqn isn't really as weather-beaten as it looks. XZ114 is one of numerous Jaguars and Harriers painted over in water-soluble whitewash camouflage for the RAF's annual winter operations deployment in Bodo, Norway. It obviously hasn't received a very good scrubbing since its return

Bottom left A lineup of Jaguars on the Deci ramp, with a 2-seat T.2 in the foreground

Below Perhaps undergoing an identity-crisis, this No 41 Sqn Jaguar T.2 carries a centreline tank decorated with the crest and checkerboard flash of its sister squadron at Coltishall, No 54 Sqn. In the foreground, the ubiquitous NATO CBLS used to mount 4-kg practice bombs

Below This Jaguar T.2A wears the distinctive tail band of No 226 Operational Conversion Unit at Lossiemouth

Bottom right A good many of the RAF Germany squadrons paid training visits to Deci during 1986. An example is this Harrier GR.3 of No 4 Sqn from Gutersloh, carrying a pair of belly-mounted 30 mm Aden cannons and a practice Sidewinder without control fins

Right Another No 4 Sqn Harrier GR.3 awaits a mission

Royal Navy Jetstream

This pair of Royal Navy No 750 Sqn Jetstream T.2s arrived at Deci after a long cross-country navigator/observer training flight from their home base at Culdrose. Starting in 1980, No 750 Sqn received 16 converted ex-RAF Jetstreams to replace its Sea Prince T.1s

RAF Hercules

With production still continuing
34 years after the flight of the
prototype in August 1954, the
C-130 Hercules is destined to be
the DC-3 of its era. Its numerous
military variants equip the air
forces of some 50 nations around
the world, with a civil version
even operating in China. This
slightly-faded Hercules C.1, the
RAF version of the C-130K,
unloads supplies after its weekly
run from RAF Lyneham

Comparison of this freshly-painted Hercules C.3 with the previous C.1 graphically illustrates the C.3's longer fuselage, which was extended some 18 feet by inserting two 'plugs' in the fuselage fore and aft of the wing. Like all RAF Hercules, this one is operated by the Air Transport Wing at Lyneham

Luftwaffe Phantoms

Below A view of the JBG-35 F-4 flight-line, with 38 + 02 being readied for a mission in the foreground. When *Luftwaffe* F-4 units visit Deci, they always come in force with 12 to 18 Phantoms instead of the usual 8 or 10 aircraft other units deploy

Bottom right This red-tailed JBG-35 F-4F carries a dayglo-orange aerial dart under its port wing. To maintain the proficiency of the 'fighter' half of their mission, *Luftwaffe* F-4 units bring along several aircraft equipped to tow targets for air-to-air gunnery practice

This Volkswagen, a modern version of the famous WW 2 'Kubelwagen,' is one of several used as staff/command vehicles by the *Luftwaffe* support unit permanently assigned at Deci

Below With a flight of four smoke-belching F-4s departing overhead, this JBG-35 Phantom has 'dropped anchor' on the Deci ramp while undergoing routine maintenance

Right This Hopsten F-4F wears a pitot cover in the colours of the German flag and shows to good advantage the frangible cap on the business end of the M61 gun under the nose

Bottom right Wearing the old-style Phantom camouflage with large insignia and buzz numbers, this F-4F from JG-74 is packing a Sidewinder missile and practice bombs for a trip to Capa Frasca. Why this F-4 from the 'Molders' fighter-interceptor squadron is on a bombing mission is a mystery

You can't keep track of the
players without a scorecard . . .
The coloured tails on this lineup
of *Luftwaffe* Phantoms help the
crews keep track of who's who
during hectic F-4 versus F-4
dogfights on the ACMI range

Far left A white tail, green stabilators and blue nose wheel door indicate this F-4F from JG-74 at Neuberg has seen a lot of air-to-air action since it replaced JG-74's F-104s in 1974

Left Quite sure the warning about the arresting hook is not meant for him, a mechanic 'gets into' his work on one of the F-4's engines

Below A JG-74 Phantom taxies out for a dart-tow mission. With the dart attached, there is not much clearance for the usual angle of attack during rotation, so the 'target tugs' must make a long, flat takeoff run

Bottom left Outfitted with practice bombs, this RF-4E is from AKG-52, a reconnaissance wing operating from Leck. Between them, AKG-52 and Bremgarten-based AKG-51 operate some 85 reconnaissance Phantoms

Left The AKG-52 emblem

Below Another AKG-52 RF-4 in the new camouflage, but still with a large German flag on the tail

A JG-71 F-4F taxies in after a
sortie on the ACMI range

This JG-71 F-4F had completed an uneventful mission on the ACMI range and was on landing rollout when it experienced a complete hydraulic failure, leaving the pilot without brakes or steering. With only a single drag chute to slow it down, the Phantom quickly ate up all of Deci's 9810-ft runway and went careening off the overrun into a farmer's field. Seeing no life-threatening danger in their situation, the very-collected crew opted to stick with the airplane as it plowed through the dirt to an eventual halt after shearing its landing gear in an irrigation ditch. Afterwards, a toast to the courageous crew, then the task of disassembling the F-4 for shipment back to Germany

Luftwaffe Starfighters

When photographed in April 1986, this F-104G was within six months of wrapping up a 25-year career in the German Navy. By the end of 1986, MFG-2 (*Marinefliegergeschwader*) at Eggebeck had converted to Tornados, most of its Starfighters being sold to Turkey. 26 + 80 is armed with underwing multiple-rocket launcher pods and a centreline practice bomb rack

Below One of Manching-based ES-61's four TF-104Gs on a weekend visit to Deci. It wears the old-style camouflage with a new green tiptank

Bottom An F-104G of JBG-34 at Memmingen. During the summer of 1986, the Italian Air Force and German *Luftwaffe* each had two squadrons of F-104s deployed to Deci. To celebrate what was to be the last deployment of an all-104 unit to Deci, the Germans instigated a mass fly-by of 35 German and Italian F-104s

When an F-104 crew chief from JBG-34 finally got his first ride in a Starfighter, he didn't quite expect it to end like this. In a borrowed TF-104G (27 + 10) visiting from ES-61 at Manching, the pilot and crew chief set off for a short aerial tour of the southern Sardinia coastline. It was an uneventful flight until on the downwind for Runway 35, they suddenly got a FIRE-ENGINE light. With no visual confirmation of a fire from other aircraft in the pattern, they tried for the runway, but as they turned base, smoke and flames started pouring from the engine. As they turned final, the 104 was a fireball and it was obvious they weren't going to make the runway. Both ejected safely, and the stricken Starfighter plunged straight into an orange grove a mile and a half from the runway and exploded. After the accident investigation, 27 + 10's remains were dumped behind the German maintenance hangar to await disposition

Luftwaffe/ Marineflieger Tornados

A clean-looking Tornado from JBG-33 at Buchel undergoes post-sortie maintenance on the line. While the beloved *Luftwaffe* F-104 could carry 7500 lbs of external ordnance, the swing-wing Tornado that replaced it can carry 18,000 lbs and has a much larger performance envelope

An unusual black and grey-camouflaged Tornado from the *Luftwaffe* test unit, ES-61, at Manching. 98 + 58 operated at Deci for a month as the launch aircraft for flight trials on a new MBB air-to-surface guided missile, which is visible on the centreline ordnance rack

Tradition and *espirit de corps* are still very strong among German units. Here, the flag of Navy strike wing MFG-1 flies over the German end of the Deci flightline. MFG-1 was the first Navy unit to replace its F-104Gs with Tornados in 1982

Below With a mechanic taking the noonday sun on the stabilator, and special-made FOD covers on the engine intakes, this Schleswig-based MFG-1 Tornado is anchored to the run-up pad for engine checks. Judging from the amount of time Italian, British and German Tornados spend on the run-up pads, their Turbo-Union RB.199 engines must require a lot of attention

Bottom One of a number of experimental camouflage schemes tried by the Navy on its strike Tornados is this 3-tone grey scheme seen on an MFG-1 Tornado taxying in at Deci in September 1985

Luftwaffe Canberra

A very rare bird. This Canberra B.2 is one of two operated by ES-61 at Manching on behalf of the Military Geographic Office. It is used as a camera platform for aerial map-making and other reconnaissance-type chores. The third B.2 (99 + 36) delivered to the *Luftwaffe* in the early sixties is now on display at an air museum in Sinsheim, West Germany

Nose view of the Canberra B.2 showing the crest of the Military Geographic Office (MGA), an RAF No 15 Sqn Tornado 'zap' and several comical examples of German nose art

Luftwaffe Transalls

Right Closeup of a Transall C-160 tail showing the emblem of the *Luftwaffe* Air Transport Command. The C-160 is another product of Franco-German partnership, the Transport Alliance. Of the first batch of 179 built to replace the Noratlas twin-boom heavy transport, 110 were delivered to the *Luftwaffe*

Below This Transall C-160D in well-worn early-style camouflage is from the Air transport command's largest unit, LTG-61 at Landsberg. Since Germany never purchased the C-130 Hercules, the Transall represents the *Luftwaffe's* entire airlift capability

Bottom right Another Landsberg-based LTG-61 Transall in the later-style camouflage and miniature-size insignia

LUFTWAFFE C-160 D65

French Air Force Mirages

The French on occasion contract training time on the ACMI range and send aircraft down to Deci. In May 1986, Mirage IIIEs and BEs from air force units at Colmar and Dijon spent a week of intensive air-to-air training at Deci. Although France withdrew her forces from the integrated allied command in 1966, the country is still committed to NATO and frequently participates in joint exercises with other members of the alliance

The Grim Reaper on the tail of
this Mirage IIIBE 2-seater is the
emblem of ECT-2/2, SPA-94, the
French Air Force's primary
Mirage training unit, based at
Dijon

Though the triangular emblem is missing from the tail, the '118' prefix to the aircraft callsign on the nose indicates this Mirage F.1 belongs to CEAM, the French Air Force's special evaluation and training unit based at Mont de Marsan. A flight of F.1s made up the second French contingent to visit Deci in 1986

French Air Force Transall

Though they have recently acquired their first C-130 Hercules transports, the French Air Transport Command consists almost entirely of Transall C-160s. This C-160A, wearing special exercise markings, was German-built by MBB and operates with transport wing ET-61 from Orleans. Along with two other Transalls, it provided airlift support for the Mirage III deployment to Deci

Swiss Air Force Mirages

Lineup of natural-metal Swiss Air Force Mirage IIISs wearing the tail emblem of No 16 Sqn at Emmen. The Mirage IIIS, 36 of which equip two squadrons, is a special variant of the Mirage built to very expensive Swiss Air Force specifications for operation from the unique highway and mountainside air bases of Switzerland

Below Carrying an ACMI instrumentation pod, this No 16 Sqn Mirage IIIS is ready for another sortie against the Alconbury Aggressors, from whom the Swiss pilots received high marks for their dogfighting skills

Bottom right One of the first Swiss Mirage IIISs to receive the new overall-grey air defence camouflage is this example from No 16 Sqn

Right Also wearing new camouflage is this Mirage IIIBS 2-seat trainer deployed to Deci with No 16 Sqn

Swiss Air Force Twin Otter

Registered HB-LID, this DHC-6 Twin Otter is used by the Swiss equivalent of the FAA for radio and NAVAID calibration checks and accompanied the Mirage deployment to Deci from its home base at Dubendorf

Swiss Air Force F-5E/F

Right Ordered in 1975 and assembled at the Swiss Federal Aircraft Factory at Emmen from components shipped from Northrop in the US, 66 single-seat E-model and 6 two-seat F-model F-5s have been delivered to Swiss Air Force squadrons. This example, in standard F-5 camoflage, is an E-model from No 13 Sqn at Meiringen

Below A two-seat F-5F of No 13 Sqn

Closeup of a Swiss Air Force
F-5E showing the No 13 Sqn
eagle emblem and the Sardinian
crest on the nose. The crest is
carried by several F-5s to
commemorate their first visit to
Deci for 'SAKA 85,' the Swiss Air
Force's air combat training
deployment